HOLME &

Easy Elegance

from Fabulous Fairholme

Breakfast · Brunch · Lunch

whitecap

Whitecap Books is known for its expertise in the cookbook market, and has produced some of the most innovative and familiar titles found in kitchens across North America. Visit our website at www.whitecap.ca.

Publisher: Michael Burch
Editor: Theresa Best
Food Preparation & Styling: Sylvia Main
Food Preparation & Assistant Styling: Mary Patterson
Food & Inn Photography: John Archer Photography
Author & Inn Photography: Cathie Ferguson Photography
Additional Photography: Ross Main
Book Design & Layout: Reber Creative

Fairholme Manor Inn website: www.fairholmemanor.com

Printed in China

Library and Archives Canada Cataloguing in Publication
Main, Sylvia
　　Easy elegance from fabulous Fairholme : breakfast, brunch, lunch / Sylvia Main.
Includes index.

ISBN 978-1-77050-110-2
　　1. Breakfasts. 2. Brunches. 3. Luncheons. 4. Fairholme Manor. 5. Cookbooks.
I. Fairholme Manor II. Title.
TX733.M374 2012　　　　　　　641.5'2　　　　　　　C2011-908319-1

The publisher acknowledges the financial support of the Government of Canada through the Canada Book Fund (CBF) and the Province of British Columbia through the Book Publishing Tax Credit.

12　13　14　15　16　　　5　4　3　2　1

Contents

Thank You

Easy Elegance from Fabulous Fairholme would have not have been possible without the support of my family and friends – along with our wonderful guests. I had so much fun with my talented team while we cooked, tested, styled, photographed and designed the cookbook. A heartfelt thank you to my team and other contributors:

Nora Pouillon
Chris Young
Mary Patterson
Sandy Reber
John and Kelly Archer
Cathie Ferguson
Erica Smolders
Sue Frause
Ross Main
Simone Main
Nicola Main
Robert McCullough
Helen Sundberg
Mary Ann Bentzon
Jason Holmes

Brasserie L'Ecole
Janet Thompson
Inge Ranzinger
Claudette Roddier
Beth von Hebel
Leah Craig
Wilf Wanke
Brendan Connell
Sean Pickersgill
Margareta Dworak
Alexander Dworak
Sandra Sanborn
Dorothee Comeau
Diane Saab
Deirdre Campbell

Metric Conversions

Volume
½ teaspoon = 2 mL
1 teaspoon = 5 mL
1 tablespoon = 15 mL
¼ cup = 60 mL
½ cup = 125 mL
¾ cup = 185 mL
1 cup = 250 mL
2 cups = 500 mL
4 cups = 1 L

Temperatures
162°F = 72°C
325°F = 160°C
350°F = 175°C
375°F = 190°C
400°F = 200°C
450°F = 230°C

Pan and Dish Sizes
8-inch (2 L) square pan
9-inch (2.5 L) square pan
9- x 13-inch (3.5 L) casserole dish

Loaf Pan Sizes
8- x 4-inch (1.5 L) loaf pan
9- x 5-inch (2 L) loaf pan

To my family, friends
and fabulous guests

Foreword

I met Sylvia Main a dozen years ago at Fairholme Manor Inn while on assignment for *Seattle* magazine. I was writing a feature on rooms with a view in British Columbia, and Fairholme Manor Inn was recommended to me. Since that first meeting, Sylvia and I have become close friends, and I continue to share her historic and elegant inn through my photographs and words.

As a travel writer, I'm often asked where is my favourite place to stay. It's Fairholme Manor, across the border in the capital city of Victoria on Vancouver Island. Fairholme is an 1885 Italianate mansion situated on a full acre in the lush Rockland area of the city. What a magical place.

What Sylvia has created at Fairholme Manor is something special. The six suites in her inn all feature clean lines, blending old and new, but never frou-frou. That carries on to her beautiful breakfasts, served elegantly in the golden-washed dining room. The first time I tasted her lemon ricotta pancakes, I was hooked.

It's no surprise that other guests are equally impressed with the delectable morning offerings – so it was only natural that Sylvia decided to write a cookbook. When she first mentioned the idea to me, I didn't hesitate, and offered to be her editor. *Fabulous Fairholme: Breakfasts & Brunches* became a Canadian best seller.

And now, cookbook number two: *Easy Elegance from Fabulous Fairholme,* the perfect follow-up to her debut cookbook. Sylvia shares not only her recipes for breakfast, brunch and lunch – but tips on style, decorating and creating what she likes to call "easy elegance." Simply put, entertaining can and should be fun and easy, achieved with minimal effort. As Sylvia says, it's all in the details – captured beautifully throughout the book in colourful images.

I'm proud and happy to be a part of Sylvia's newest cookbook. It was a labour of love, filled with friendship and laughter. And best of all, you can take Fairholme Manor home with you, no matter where you live. So come inside, take a peek, and experience *Easy Elegance from Fabulous Fairholme.*

Sue Frause

Introduction

When *Fabulous Fairholme: Breakfasts & Brunches* was published, I had no idea that a second cookbook would evolve four years later. So it did, and *Easy Elegance from Fabulous Fairholme* has arrived. My husband, Ross, and I have hosted guests from around the world since we opened Fairholme Manor Inn in 1999, and I know that entertaining isn't always simple and stress free. But it can be, as well as fun and creative. Within the pages of this cookbook you'll find easy-to-prepare recipes, menus, decorating and style tips and even ideas for making simple gifts from the kitchen. All achieved with minimal effort, all ideas that can be incorporated into your lifestyle. Easy. Elegant. Delicious.

There's nothing I enjoy more than sharing a lovely meal around the table with my family and friends – add a dash of lively conversation and plenty of laughter, and you have the perfect get-together. But people today lead busy lives, leaving little time to cook and prepare meals for loved ones. And then there's the misconception that entertaining is a chore – it doesn't need to be. I like to create simple menus that both look and taste special, and the table setting adds to the magic. Whether it's a small bouquet of fresh flowers from your garden, or colourful glassware and unique serving containers, simple touches can add zest to your dining experience. It's all in the details.

As for the food, creating easy and elegant dishes begins with the ingredients. It's most important to use fresh produce, locally sourced if possible. Better yet, grow your own! And don't forget that something as simple as garnishing a dish with fresh herbs or edible flowers from your garden adds the perfect finishing touch to any meal.

I'm fortunate to be able to share recipes from two highly regarded chefs. Celebrated chef Nora Pouillon is my cousin and the owner of Restaurant Nora in Washington, DC – the first certified organic restaurant in the United States. Seattle chef Chris Young, who co-authored the widely acclaimed *Modernist Cuisine: The Art and Science of Cooking*, has been a guest at Fairholme Manor over the years and held his wedding brunch here. I welcome their creative contributions!

A fun feature of the cookbook is *Little Gifts from the Kitchen*, which showcases simple ways to create hostess gifts incorporating your own creations for unique and personalized gift giving. There is also a trio of easy and elegant menus to give you inspiration for easy breakfast, brunch and lunch entertaining.

A word about travel – bring it home with you. I spent time in four of my favourite cities in the past few years: New York, Paris, Venice and Vienna. And wherever I was, there were opportunities to pick up special items for home entertaining, from the coloured glassware in Venice to the heart-shaped sugar cubes I found in a Viennese shop. Save space in your suitcase for your travel finds, and then share them at the table with your family and friends.

I hope you enjoy *Easy Elegance from Fabulous Fairholme*. Happy Cooking! Bon Appetit! Buon Appetito! Guten Appetit!

Sylvia

Sylvia Main

Easy. Elegant. Delicious.

Fairholme Maple-Pecan Granola

MAKES 8 CUPS

3 cups	quick oats
½ cup	wheat germ
1 cup	wheat bran
½ cup	oat bran
1 cup	unsweetened coconut, shredded
¼ cup	flax seeds
½ cup	pistachios, coarsely chopped
½ cup	sunflower seeds, raw
1 cup	almonds, sliced
2 tablespoons	cinnamon
½ teaspoon	salt
½ cup	vegetable oil
¼ cup	water
1 cup	maple syrup or honey
1 tablespoon	pure vanilla
½ cup	pecans, halved
1 cup	dried cranberries, blueberries or sour cherries
½ cup	dried apricots

At Fairholme we often leave the baked granola overnight in the turned-off oven. This makes an extra crunchy granola. Remove from oven and break into bite-sized pieces.

Preheat oven to 250°F. Line two large baking sheets with parchment paper.

Mix together the first 11 ingredients in a large bowl. In a separate bowl, whisk together oil, water, maple syrup or honey and vanilla. Add to dry ingredients and mix together thoroughly.

Divide the mixture between the two baking sheets and pack down. Sprinkle top with pecans but do not mix as you want the pecans to toast. Bake 1 hour. Turn off oven and do not disturb!

Leave granola in oven until cooled, about 45 minutes, to ensure crunchiness. When cooled, mix in dried fruit and store in an airtight container.

Serve with vanilla yoghurt, Greek yoghurt or milk and fresh fruit.

Breakfast Granola Cookies

MAKES 3 DOZEN COOKIES

Breakfast to go!

1 cup	butter, softened
1 cup	brown sugar
2 teaspoons	pure vanilla
2	eggs, beaten
2 cups	whole wheat flour
2 teaspoons	baking soda
4 cups	Fairholme Maple-Pecan Granola (page 5)

Preheat oven to 350°F.

Cream butter and brown sugar. Add vanilla and eggs and combine. Stir in flour and baking soda, then fold in granola. Make 3 dozen balls from mixture. Flatten the balls and place onto greased or parchment-lined baking sheets.

Use two baking sheets together to prevent the bottoms of the cookies from becoming too brown. Bake for about 12 minutes. Cool and store tightly covered.

Apricot-Coconut Granola Bars

MAKES 1 DOZEN BARS

2 cups	old fashioned oats
½ cup	brown sugar
¼ cup	maple syrup
1 cup	all-purpose flour
1 cup	unsweetened coconut, shredded
1 teaspoon	pure vanilla
½ teaspoon	baking soda
1	egg
¼ cup	water
½ cup	vegetable oil
¾ cup	dried apricots, diced
½ cup	dried cranberries or sour cherries
½ cup	chocolate chips, semisweet or milk

Preheat oven to 375°F. Line a 9- x 13-inch baking pan with parchment paper or foil.

Mix together all ingredients. Press into the prepared pan. Bake 30–35 minutes until golden. While still warm cut into 12 squares. Store tightly covered for up to 2 weeks.

Great as an energy bar or for kids' lunches.

Individual Baby Potato, Cheese, Bacon & Thyme Frittatas

MAKES 6 INDIVIDUAL FRITTATAS

6 slices	bacon
8 large	eggs
3 additional	egg whites
½ cup	milk
½ teaspoon	salt
½ teaspoon	pepper
3 tablespoons	green onion, thinly chopped
½ cup	Gruyère cheese, shredded
2 teaspoon	fresh thyme, minced
1½ cups	baby potatoes, steamed and halved
¼ cup	Parmesan cheese, grated
small block	Parmesan cheese, shaved, to serve (optional)

Choosing the right potato is key to this recipe. Use baby Yukon Gold potatoes or baby red potatoes, not baking potatoes such as russet.

Preheat oven to 350°F. Grease 6 ramekins.

In a skillet, cook bacon until almost crisp. Place bacon on a paper towel and set aside.

Whisk together eggs, egg whites, milk, salt and pepper. Add green onion, grated Gruyère cheese and thyme. Divide the potatoes and bacon between the ramekins then pour egg mixture over them. Sprinkle with Parmesan cheese.

Bake for about 30 minutes (or refrigerate overnight and bake the next morning for about 35 minutes). Frittatas should be puffy around the edges and tester should come out clean. Allow frittatas to rest for 5 minutes before serving. Remove from ramekins.

To make Parmesan curls for garnish, just shave the Parmesan block with a vegetable peeler.

Serve with warm bread, scones and extra bacon for breakfast, brunch or lunch.

Roasted Vegetable & Three-Cheese Frittata

SERVES 6

1	yellow pepper, cubed
1	red pepper, cubed
½	red onion, cubed
1 teaspoon	olive oil
1 clove	garlic, minced
8 large	eggs
3 additional	egg whites
½ cup	milk
½ cup	Gouda cheese, shredded
½ cup	cheddar, shredded
½ teaspoon	salt
1 tablespoon	fresh thyme or basil, finely chopped
¼ cup	Parmesan cheese, grated

When broiling, leave the oven door ajar to prevent burning the cheese.

Preheat oven to 350°F. Toss the peppers and onion with the olive oil. Roast on a parchment-lined baking sheet in oven for 20 minutes. Sprinkle the garlic over vegetables and continue roasting for about another 10 minutes.

Whisk together the eggs, egg whites, milk, Gouda, cheddar and salt. Add the roasted vegetables and thyme to the egg mixture. Pour mixture into a buttered 8-inch frying pan on medium to high heat. Use a spatula to fold the egg mixture under sides of frittata as if preparing an omelette. This should take 5 minutes.

Place pan into the oven for frittata to set, about 10 minutes. Remove pan from oven. Set oven temperature to broil. Sprinkle frittata with Parmesan cheese. Place in oven under broiler until frittata puffs up and the cheese is lightly browned, about 2 minutes.

Give the pan a little shake to ensure that the egg is set in the middle. Remove from oven and cut the frittata into 6 wedges.

Serve with smoked salmon, smoked tuna or bacon, or with warm bread and a crisp salad. Feel free to substitute other vegetables in the frittata such as zucchini, eggplant and asparagus.

Parmesan Cheese Sautéed Potatoes

SERVES 4–6

These potatoes are a great side dish for breakfast, brunch or lunch.

24	small new or baby potatoes, halved
4 tablespoons	olive oil
1 teaspoon	lemon zest
4 tablespoons	Parmesan cheese, grated
3 teaspoons	fresh flat-leaf parsley, chopped
1 teaspoon	salt
dash	pepper
dash	cayenne

Heat oil in large, heavy skillet or griddle over medium-high heat. Add potatoes and sauté for 8–10 minutes until golden. Add the lemon zest and 1 tablespoon Parmesan cheese.

Cook for 1 minute, stirring, then add another tablespoon of Parmesan cheese. (Keep adding the Parmesan cheese a spoonful at a time to prevent the cheese from burning.) Keep stirring!

Stir in the parsley and season with salt, pepper and cayenne.

Spinach Ricotta Cups

2 tablespoons	olive oil
2 cloves	garlic, finely chopped
2 cups	fresh spinach, packed and chopped
1½ cups	ricotta cheese
2	eggs, slightly beaten
½ cup	Parmesan cheese, grated
2 tablespoons	fresh chives or basil, chopped
¼ cup	pine nuts, toasted
dash	cayenne
dash	salt

Preheat oven to 400°F. Grease 4 large ramekins.

In a skillet, sauté garlic in the oil over low heat until translucent, about 3 minutes. Add spinach and cook, covered, for a couple of minutes until wilted.

In a bowl, combine ricotta, eggs, Parmesan cheese, chives and pine nuts. Fold in spinach mixture along with cayenne and salt. Divide among the prepared ramekins.

Bake uncovered for 20–25 minutes or until ricotta cups are firm.

Serve with Pan-Roasted Cherry Tomatoes (page 19) and Parmesan Cheese Sautéed Potatoes (page 12).

Herb & Cheddar Scrambled Egg Strudel

SERVES 6

12	eggs, beaten
½ cup	light cream
dash	cayenne
½ teaspoon	salt
2 tablespoons	butter
2 tablespoons	fresh herbs, chopped (chives, parsley, tarragon)
2 tablespoons	cream cheese
½ cup	cheddar cheese, shredded
6 sheets	phyllo pastry
3 tablespoons	butter, melted
18	asparagus spears, ends removed
dash	salt
dash	pepper
1 tablespoon	olive oil

For a variation, substitute julienned prosciutto ham (with fat removed) for the herbs.

Crack eggs into a bowl. Add cream, cayenne and salt. Whisk eggs vigorously for 2 minutes to incorporate air into mixture.

Heat a non-stick skillet over medium heat and melt butter. In skillet, slowly cook the eggs, using a spatula to gently fold raw eggs under. Do not rush and "stir" the eggs. Do not overcook; eggs should still be moist. Add herbs and cheeses. Set aside.

Preheat oven to 375°F.

Use 2 phyllo sheets. Brush 1 sheet with melted butter then top with second buttered sheet. Place ⅙ of the scrambled egg mixture at the bottom of sheet and roll up with both sides tucked in about 3 inches either side. Continue making 5 more strudels. Bake on parchment-lined baking sheet for about 15–20 minutes or until golden brown.

While strudels are baking, prepare asparagus. Place asparagus onto parchment-lined baking sheet. Drizzle olive oil over asparagus and season with salt and pepper. Roast for about 8 minutes.

Serve one strudel per person with three roasted asparagus spears or Pan-Roasted Cherry Tomatoes (page 19) on the side.

Pan-Roasted Cherry Tomatoes

SERVES 4–6

1 tablespoon	olive oil
4 cups	cherry tomatoes, mixed red and yellow
2 cloves	garlic, minced
1 tablespoon	fresh basil or oregano, chopped
¼ teaspoon	salt
dash	sugar
dash	chili pepper flakes
2 tablespoons	green onion, thinly sliced
1–2 teaspoons	balsamic vinegar

This is delicious paired with any egg dish, such as Ham and Cheese Cups or Herb and Cheese Scrambled Egg Strudel.

In a large skillet, heat oil over medium-high heat. Add cherry tomatoes, garlic, basil, salt, sugar, chili pepper flakes and green onion. Sauté for about 3–5 minutes. Stir in balsamic vinegar.

Baked Eggs in Ham Cups

SERVES 4

This recipe is easy, elegant and so delicious, but also an excellent everday dish for kids!

You can use large muffin tins in place of ramekins.

4 thin slices	smoked ham or any deli ham
4	eggs
4 tablespoons	cheddar or mozzarella cheese, shredded
2	green onions or chives, finely chopped
dash	salt
dash	pepper

Preheat oven to 350°F. Grease 4 ramekins.

Line each ramekin with a slice of ham to create a cup. Sprinkle cheese into each ham-lined ramekin. Break 1 egg gently into each ramekin. Sprinkle with green onion, salt and pepper.

Bake for about 15–20 minutes until whites are just set but yolks are still a bit runny and ham is crispy on the edges.

Serve with hot buttered toast or Parmesan Cheese Sautéed Potatoes (page 12).

Individual Cheese & Herb Soufflés

SERVES 6

¼ cup	butter
¼ cup	all-purpose flour
1 cup	milk
dash	salt
dash	pepper
dash	cayenne
2 tablespoons	fresh mixed herbs (parsley, chives, tarragon, thyme or basil)
¾ cup	cheddar cheese, shredded
¼ cup	Parmesan cheese, grated
3	eggs, separated

Preheat oven to 375°F. Grease 6 ramekins.

In a skillet, melt butter over low heat. Add flour slowly with a whisk until fully incorporated. Turn up heat to medium and cook for about 3 minutes. Slowly whisk the milk into the butter and flour mixture. Turn off heat and add the salt, pepper, cayenne, herbs and cheeses, then whisk in the yolks. Set the herb and cheese sauce aside.

Beat egg whites until stiff. Gently fold egg whites into the herb and cheese mixture. Divide the mixture between the ramekins and bake for 20–25 minutes.

Serve immediately with warm bread and a crisp salad for an elegant brunch or lunch.

Variations

Spinach, Cheese & Herb Soufflé
Sauté 3 cups packed, chopped spinach in 1 tablespoon olive oil. Add to the herb and cheese sauce. Continue with recipe.

Ham, Cheese & Herb Soufflé
Add ¾ cup cubed ham to the herb and cheese sauce. Continue with recipe.

Mini Potato & Spring Onion Pancakes

SERVES 4–6

2	large russet or Yukon Gold potatoes, peeled and cubed
3	eggs, separated
¼ cup	sour cream
2 tablespoons	all-purpose flour
½ teaspoon	salt
½ cup	frozen corn
2 tablespoons	green onion, thinly chopped
dash	coarse pepper for garnish

This recipe works well with leftover mashed potatoes – substitute 2 cups of mashed potatoes for the recipe potatoes.

Boil potatoes until tender. Drain and mash thoroughly. Add the egg yolks, sour cream, flour, salt, corn and green onion to the mashed potatoes. Beat egg whites until stiff and pour into the potato mixture.

Heat oil in a large skillet on medium-low heat. Drop 3–4 tablespoons of batter into the skillet to form a pancake. Flip the pancakes after about 2 minutes or when golden.

At Fairholme we serve three of these mini pancakes on a plate with various toppings.

Topping Variations

Smoked salmon and Lemon Crème Fraîche (page 119)

Poached egg and blanched asparagus

Sautéed crimini mushrooms and Quick Crème Fraîche (page 119)

Pan-Roasted Cherry Tomatoes (page 19)

Potato Latkes

4 large	russet potatoes, washed and peeled
1½ medium	yellow onions, finely sliced
2 tablespoons	green onion or chives, chopped
¼ cup	all-purpose flour
2	eggs, beaten
1 teaspoon	salt
½ teaspoon	pepper
dash	cayenne
½ teaspoon	nutmeg
½ teaspoon	cumin
	sunflower or vegetable oil (for frying)

Preheat oven to 350°F.

In a food processor or with a grater, shred the potatoes and onions. Mix potatoes and onions together in a bowl and squeeze out excess liquid. Add remaining ingredients, except the oil, and mix well.

Heat oil in a large skillet over medium heat. When oil is hot, drop 4–6 rounded tablespoons of the mixture into the skillet and flatten slightly. Cook for about 8 minutes. Flip and continue other side until latkes are golden and edges are crisp. Cook the latkes slowly and evenly to ensure crispness.

Drain on paper towels or rack. Place latkes back in pan and finish in oven for about 5 minutes.

Serve with sour cream or Lemon Crème Fraîche (page 119).

Variation

Substitute yam or a carrot and potato blend for potato.

Creamy Crimini Mushroom Phyllo Cups

SERVES 6

Using phyllo can be tricky so work quickly! Keep pastry covered with a damp tea towel while you are working with it.

1 tablespoon	butter
1½ cups	crimini or small mushrooms, finely sliced
1 tablespoon	olive oil
2 cloves	garlic, crushed
1 tablespoon	fresh thyme or Italian parsley
½ cup	goat cheese or cream cheese
1	egg
2	egg yolks
½ cup	Quick Crème Fraîche (page 119)
2 tablespoons	butter, melted
3	phyllo pastry sheets

Preheat oven to 425°F.

Heat the oil and 1 tablespoon of butter in a frying pan over medium-high heat. Add mushrooms and sauté for about 3 minutes. Add garlic and thyme, then sauté quickly. Be careful not to burn garlic. Set aside.

In a bowl, mix together half the cheese and the sautéed mushrooms. Set aside. In a separate bowl, mix together the rest of the cheese, the egg, egg yolks and Quick Crème Fraîche. Combine the two mixtures. Set aside.

Melt the 2 tablespoons of butter in a small pot. Brush one sheet of phyllo with melted butter. Top with another sheet and brush with butter. Repeat with the remaining sheet. Cut stack into six 4-inch squares. Press into buttered muffin tins.

Spoon the mushroom mixture into each phyllo-lined muffin tin.

Bake about 20 minutes until golden and set. Garnish with a dollop of Quick Crème Fraîche (optional).

Serve with bacon, sausages or smoked salmon, or alone with a crisp green salad.

Raspberry Upside-Down Buttermilk Pancakes

SERVES 4–6

2 cups	all-purpose flour
2 teaspoons	baking powder
1 teaspoon	baking soda
3 tablespoons	sugar
dash	salt
2	eggs, lightly beaten
zest	1 orange or lemon
3 cups	buttermilk
4 tablespoons	butter, melted
1 cup	fresh or frozen raspberries, blackberries, cranberries or blueberries
½ cup	white chocolate chips to garnish
½ cup	fresh raspberries to garnish
	icing sugar to serve

Preheat lightly oiled griddle or skillet over medium-low heat.

Sift together the flour, baking powder, baking soda, sugar and salt. Add the lightly beaten eggs, zest, buttermilk and butter. The batter should be slightly lumpy.

For each pancake pour ½ cup of batter on the griddle or skillet, leaving about an inch of space between the pancakes. Distribute the berries over the pancakes. When bubbles begin to appear on top, flip over each pancake and continue to cook until golden brown.

To serve, sprinkle with white chocolate chips, extra raspberries and icing sugar. Top with maple syrup or whipped cream if desired.

For a more decadent pancake, throw in a handful of white chocolate chips to the batter. So delicious!

Overnight Belgian Waffles with Hazelnuts

SERVES 4

2 cups	all-purpose flour
1 teaspoon	yeast
1 tablespoon	sugar
½ teaspoon	salt
2 cups	milk
6 tablespoons	butter, melted
1	egg
1 teaspoon	pure vanilla
½ cup	hazelnuts or pecans, chopped and lightly toasted

In place of nuts, you can use ½ cup of blueberries and 1 teaspoon orange or lemon zest. To prevent blueberries from burning in the waffle iron, layer half the batter, add the blueberries and then cover with the remaining batter.

In a bowl, combine the flour, yeast, sugar and salt. Gently stir in the milk, butter, egg and vanilla. Cover the bowl tightly with plastic wrap. Refrigerate overnight.

In the morning, fold the hazelnuts into the batter. Heat a lightly oiled waffle iron. Pour ¾ cup of batter onto preheated waffle iron. Close lid and cook waffles for about 4–5 minutes, until steam stops.

Topping options include Honey Butter (page 123), Warm Bumbleberry Coulis or Strawberry Syrup (both on page 118). Or simply sprinkle with icing sugar and serve with maple syrup on the side.

Ricotta Blintzes with Strawberry Syrup

SERVES 6

For the crêpes

1 cup	all-purpose flour
2	large eggs
1 cup	milk
dash	salt
2 teaspoons	sugar
1 teaspoon	vegetable oil or melted butter

For the filling

3 cups	fresh ricotta cheese (or cottage cheese)
3 tablespoons	maple syrup or ¼ cup sugar
1 tablespoon	lemon zest or 1 teaspoon cinnamon
	icing sugar to serve

To make the crêpes, whisk together flour, eggs, milk, salt, sugar and vegetable oil until smooth. Place batter in refrigerator for at least 1 hour or overnight.

Heat lightly oiled non-stick skillet or crêpe pan over medium heat. Pour one medium ladle of batter onto the pan and swirl to cover entire pan.

Cook briefly and flip over with a wide spatula. Continue to cook until golden, about 1–2 minutes. Make sure the pan comes up to temperature between crêpes. Layer crêpes between parchment paper or plastic wrap to keep them from sticking together.

To make the filling, mix together the ricotta, maple syrup and lemon zest.

Preheat oven to 350°F. Line baking sheet with parchment paper. Spread ½ cup of filling onto the centre of each of the crêpes. Fold each crêpe to form a rectangular package. Place the blintzes on the cookie sheet, seams down. Bake until hot, about 5 minutes.

Sprinkle blintzes with icing sugar. Serve with warm Strawberry Syrup (page 118), on the side or poured over the blintzes. Also great with maple syrup.

Cooking with Chris Young

I first met Sylvia when my girlfriend and I spent a weekend in Victoria and stayed at Fairholme Manor. What a fantastic place! Shortly after that visit, I moved from Seattle to London to work with Heston Blumental and to open and run The Fat Duck Experimental Kitchen.

Over the years I've stayed in touch with Sylvia; indeed, I married my girlfriend, Dawn, in Victoria and we spent the night of our wedding at Fairholme Manor. Sylvia put on a wonderful breakfast for our friends and families the next morning. Needless to say, when Sylvia asked if I would be willing to contribute some recipes to her latest book from my book *Modernist Cuisine: The Art and Science of Cooking*, I happily obliged. Although my style of cooking is more common in professional kitchens, all of these recipes can easily be done at home.

Bacon Jam

MAKES APPROX 1½ CUPS

2½ tablespoons	glucose syrup
2 tablespoons	sugar
2 tablespoons	water
2 tablespoons	dark amber maple syrup
4 yolks	egg yolks
½ cup	rendered bacon fat, warm
6–8 slices	bacon
	salt to taste

Glucose syrup is half as sweet as sugar and is used to make the recipe less sweet. Isomalt is another low-sweet sugar, available at some health food stores, that can be used as a substitute.

Combine the glucose syrup, sugar, water, and maple syrup. Heat until sugar fully dissolves, then set aside to cool. Blend egg yolks into cool syrup and heat slowly while whisking constantly until the mixture becomes thick and syrupy – about 175°F.

Once the egg-syrup mixture thickens, slowly drizzle the bacon fat into the mixture while whisking. Pour the mixture into a blender and blend until it becomes a lighter colour and thicker. Pour into a medium-sized bowl.

Bake the bacon in a 350°F oven until crispy, about 30 minutes. Blot the excess oil off the bacon with paper towels. Cool and then cut or break into small pieces.

Fold bacon into the jam. Season with salt to taste. Refrigerate until needed (up to 1 month).

Photo at left: Thanks to my daughter Nicola for helping to wash the dishes.

French-Style Scrambled Eggs

SERVES 4

For the whipped eggs

8	egg yolks from large eggs
4	egg whites
4 tablespoons	unsalted butter, melted
4 tablespoons	whole milk
1 teaspoon	salt

For the garnish

sherry vinegar to taste
maple syrup as needed (about ¼ cup)
maldon or similar flaky sea salt
fresh, coarse ground pepper
finely sliced chives

Separate the yolks from the egg whites. In a bowl, combine 8 yolks with 4 egg whites, and blend until smooth. Pour into a heat-resistant plastic bag (e.g., a Ziplock bag). Squeeze out all of the air and seal the bag.

Using a digital thermometer to check, bring a large pot of water up to 162°F. Place the plastic bag with the egg mixture into the pot of water, and turn the heat beneath the pot to the lowest setting. Adjust the burner as needed to hold the temperature between 160°F and 165°F while cooking the egg mixture for 25 minutes. The egg mixture will thicken.

Pour the eggs into a blender, along with the melted unsalted butter, milk and salt. Blend until creamy.

Transfer the thickened, warm egg mixture into a whipping cream siphon. Hold the siphon upside down (and over the sink just in case of a leak) and charge the siphon with 3 whipped cream chargers. Keep the whipping siphon hot in the pot of water until needed.

To serve

Blend a small amount of sherry vinegar into a small amount of maple syrup to taste. The acidity of the sherry vinegar should just balance the sweetness of the maple syrup.

Fill a warm egg cup with the whipped eggs. Drizzle some of the sweet and sour maple syrup over the egg. Sprinkle a small amount of salt, pepper and chives overtop.

Serve with toast points.

Strawberry Gazpacho

SERVES 4

For the gazpacho

2¼ cups	strawberries, sliced and finely diced
½ cup	cucumber, peeled, seeded and finely diced
½ cup	red bell pepper, charred, peeled and finely sliced
½ cup	sweet onions, thinly sliced and finely diced
1 clove	garlic, crushed
3 tablespoons	olive oil
2 tablespoons	white balsamic vinegar
1 tablespoon	balsamic vinegar
1 tablespoon	fresh lime juice
	white balsamic vinegar to taste
dash	pepper
dash	salt

For the strawberry consommé

1¾ cups	strawberries
1 tablespoon	sugar (or fructose)

For the garnish

6	strawberries, hulled and finely diced
⅓ bunch	fresh chives, finely minced
1	red bell pepper, finely diced
½	English cucumber, peeled, seeded and finely diced
1–2 tablespoons	high-quality imported almond oil or other nut oil
4 sprigs	fresh chervil

continued on next page

To make the gazpacho

The day before serving, mix together strawberries, cucumber, bell pepper, onion, garlic, olive oil, 2 tablespoons white balsamic vinegar and 1 tablespoon balsamic vinegar in a large bowl. Season with salt and pepper. Cover with plastic wrap and transfer to refrigerator. Let chill overnight.

Next day, make the strawberry consommé. Thinly slice the strawberries and place into a bowl. Toss with sugar (or fructose, which will bring out the strawberry flavour better). Cover and let sit for 2 hours at room temperature. Decant off the juice and reserve.

Transfer chilled gazpacho mixture to the jar of a blender; blend until smooth. Blend in the reserved strawberry consommé to thin the texture of the soup. Season to taste with fresh lime juice, white balsamic vinegar, pepper and salt. Chill in the refrigerator.

To make the garnish

Place strawberries, chives, bell pepper, cucumber, and almond oil in a medium bowl; gently toss to combine.

Divide garnish evenly between four bowls. Ladle chilled gazpacho around garnish in bowls. Drizzle a little more almond oil over the garnish and gazpacho. Add a sprig of chervil and serve immediately.

Variation

You can substitute raspberries for the strawberries. You may need to season to taste with slightly less vinegar depending on how tart the raspberries are.

When we think of gazpacho, most of us think of tomatoes. The soup, however, is older than the European arrival of the tomato in the 16th century. Numerous variations, both ancient and modern, exist of this simple chilled soup. This recipe is an adaptation from a version created by one of my favourite chefs, David Kinch of Manresa. In most recipes, the acidity of the tomato fruit provides a nice balance between sweet and tart; why not, he thought, use another fruit with similar qualities? Strawberry gazpacho is now one of his signature dishes.

Sprouted Grain Bread

YIELDS 2 LOAVES

Bond Bond's Bakery, established in 1992, serves Victorians artisan breads and pastries made from scratch using traditional recipes, natural ingredients and a hands-on approach. The owners, bakers Jeneen and Richard Harrison, are passionate about maintaining old bakery favourites as well as creating new items to excite their loyal customers and entice new ones! Here is their three-part recipe.

For the starter

2¼ cups all-purpose flour
1½ cups cold water
¼ teaspoon dry yeast
  or ½ teaspoon fresh yeast

Combine flour, water and yeast in a container and stir until combined. Cover and allow to sit at room temperature for 18–22 hours.

For the grains

¼ cup flax seeds
¼ cup cracked wheat
½ cup warm water

Combine the grains and water. Let sit at room temperature for 4 hours, then refrigerate overnight or until ready to make the bread.

For the dough

3 cups all-purpose flour
2½ tablespoons dark rye flour
1 tablespoon salt
¾ teaspoon dry yeast
  or 1½ teaspoons fresh yeast
½ cup olive oil
1⅓ cup warm water

In a mixer with a dough attachment, add the starter, the grain mixture and all the dough ingredients at the same time. Mix on high speed for 4 to 5 minutes, scraping the bowl sides every minute. Place dough in a lightly oiled bowl. Cover with plastic wrap and let rest for 1½ hours at room temperature. Punch down the dough, folding each side back into the centre. Return to bowl, cover again and let rise again for 1½ hours.

Place dough onto a heavily floured surface and lightly punch and fold into a rectangular shape, approximately 8 x 11 inches. Allow to rest covered for 1 hour, then gently divide in half with a sharp knife.

Place onto a baking sheet cut-side up. Bake at 475°F for 20 to 25 minutes. For a darker crust, bake an extra 3 to 5 minutes.

We serve this fabulous bread at Fairholme hot out of the oven with our favourite jams.

Chive & Black Pepper Popovers

MAKES 12 MINI POPOVERS

1½ tablespoons	butter, melted, plus more to grease the mini muffin or popover tins
1½ cups	all-purpose flour
¼ teaspoon	pepper
large dash	salt
3	eggs
1½ cups	milk
2 tablespoons	chives, chopped in ¼-inch pieces

Preheat oven to 425°F.

Place all ingredients, except the chives, in a blender and pulse to mix well. Stir in chives.

Heat greased mini muffin or popover tins in oven for 2 minutes. Remove and fill the hot tins to the top with the popover mixture.

Bake for 20 minutes without peeking in the oven.

Serve hot as an alternative to bread.

Variation

Cinnamon Sugar Popovers

Omit chopped chives and pepper.

When the popovers are still hot, brush them with 2 tablespoons of melted butter, and place in a bowl. Combine 1 teaspoon cinnamon and ½ cup granulated sugar and pour over popovers. Toss to coat.

Kids love cinnamon sugar popovers!

Blueberry Caramel Cinnamon Buns

SERVES 12

For the dough		
	3 cups	all-purpose flour
	2 tablespoons	sugar
	1 tablespoon	baking powder
	½ teaspoon	baking soda
	⅔ cup	cold butter, in pieces
	1½ cups	buttermilk
For the filling		
	¼ cup	butter, melted
	¾ cup	brown sugar
	1 tablespoon	cinnamon
	½ cup	blueberries, fresh or frozen
	1 cup	pecans, chopped
For the caramel		
	4 tablespoons	butter, melted
	1 cup	brown sugar
	½ cup	half and half cream

Instead of blueberries, use raisins for easy raisin caramel cinnamon buns.

Preheat oven to 375°F.

Dough

In a bowl, mix the flour, sugar, baking powder and baking soda. Blend in the cold butter until mixture resembles coarse crumbs. Add the buttermilk and mix briefly to form a dough. On a lightly floured surface, roll out dough into an 18- x 12-inch rectangle.

Filling

Brush dough with the melted butter. Then sprinkle with brown sugar, cinnamon, blueberries and pecans. Starting with the edge closest to you, roll dough into a jelly-roll shape. With a serrated knife, cut into 12 pinwheels.

Caramel

Melt the butter in a saucepan. Whisk in brown sugar and cream. Cook the mixture for 5–8 minutes until smooth. Pour into a 9-inch pie plate. Sprinkle pecans over the caramel.

Lay the 12 pinwheels cut-side up on the caramel. Bake for about 45 minutes and remove from oven.

Cool for 5 minutes, then invert the cinnamon buns onto a deep serving dish.

Double-Cheese Muffins

MAKES 12 MINI MUFFINS OR 8 MEDIUM MUFFINS

1 cup	all-purpose flour
1 teaspoon	baking powder
dash	cayenne
2	eggs
1¼ cups	buttermilk
3 tablespoons	butter, melted
4	green onions, chopped (optional)
3 tablespoons	Parmesan cheese, grated
½ cup	cheddar, shredded

Preheat oven to 350°F. Grease muffin tins.

Combine flour, baking powder and cayenne in a bowl.

In a separate bowl, whisk together eggs, buttermilk, butter and green onions. Gently fold wet ingredients into dry. Fold in the two cheeses.

Spoon into muffins tins. Bake mini muffins for about 15–18 minutes and medium muffins 20–25 minutes.

Great with any soup.

Cranberry Walnut Scones

MAKES 16 SCONES

3 cups	all-purpose flour
⅓ cup	sugar
1 tablespoon	baking powder
½ teaspoon	baking soda
dash	salt
1 teaspoon	cinnamon
zest	1 orange
¾ cup	cold butter, cut in 1-inch cubes
1 cup	cranberries, dried
½ cup	walnuts or pecans, chopped
1¼ cup	buttermilk
2 tablespoons	raw sugar
½ teaspoon	cinnamon

Preheat oven to 350°F.

Combine the flour, sugar, baking powder, baking soda, salt, cinnamon
and orange zest in a bowl or food processor. Add the butter cubes into the
flour mixture and mix with a fork or in a food processor until the mixture
resembles coarse peas. Mix in the cranberries, walnuts and buttermilk.
Turn out the dough onto a lightly floured surface.

Halve the dough and form 2 rounds. Pat each round into 1-inch thickness.
Cut 8 pieces out of each round. Place scones on a parchment-lined or
well-greased baking sheet. Blend together raw sugar and cinnamon and
sprinkle onto scone tops.

Use 2 baking sheets together to prevent the bottom of the scones from
becoming too brown. Bake for about 20 minutes or until golden brown.

*Serve with Lemon-Orange Curd (page 126) or Lemon Crème Fraîche
(page 119).*

Maple Scones

3 cups	all-purpose flour
1 tablespoon	baking powder
½ teaspoon	baking soda
dash	salt
¾ cup	cold butter, cut in 1-inch cubes
1	egg
½ cup	maple syrup
⅓ cup	buttermilk
1½ teaspoons	pure vanilla
	raw sugar for garnish

To make this decadent scone even richer just add ½ cup of dark chocolate chips to the buttermilk stage of the above method.

Preheat oven to 350°F.

Combine the flour, baking powder, baking soda and salt in a bowl or food processor. Add the butter cubes and mix until the butter resembles coarse crumbs.

In a separate bowl, stir together egg, maple syrup, buttermilk and vanilla.

Add egg mixture to the flour mixture and work until a dough forms, adding a little extra buttermilk if the dough is too stiff. Do not overmix.

Turn out the dough onto a lightly floured surface. Roll out the dough ¾-inch thick. Cut out 30 small hearts or 12 large rounds.

Place the scones onto a parchment-lined or well-greased baking sheet. Use two baking sheets together to prevent the bottoms of the scones from becoming too brown. Sprinkle scone tops with raw sugar. Bake heart-shaped scones for about 15 minutes and large round scones for 20–25 minutes or until golden brown.

Serve with Bacon Jam (page 39) or Pumpkin Spice Spread (page 127).

Lemon White-Chocolate Raw Sugar Scones

MAKES 12 LARGE SCONES OR 18 MINI SCONES

3 cups	all-purpose flour
3 tablespoons	sugar
2 tablespoons	baking powder
¼ teaspoon	salt
zest	1 lemon
¾ cup	cold butter, cut in 1-inch cubes
1	egg
1 cup (approximately)	buttermilk or sour cream
½ cup	white chocolate chips
	raw sugar for garnish

Preheat oven to 375°F.

Combine flour, sugar, baking powder, salt, lemon zest and butter cubes in a bowl or food processor. Mix or pulse until mixture resembles coarse peas. Crack the egg into a large glass measuring cup and beat lightly. Add sour cream or buttermilk until the liquid reaches 9 ounces. Slowly add the liquid mixture to the flour mixture. Be careful not to overmix. This helps to create a light, flaky scone.

continued on next page

Turn out dough onto lightly floured surface. Gently fold in white chocolate chips. Pat or roll out the dough to a 1-inch thickness. Using a 3-inch round cookie cutter for larger scones or a 1½-inch round cookie cutter for mini scones, cut dough into shapes and place on parchment-lined baking sheet. Use 2 baking sheets together to prevent the bottoms of the scones from becoming too brown.

Sprinkle tops of scones generously with raw sugar. Bake large scones for about 15–20 minutes and mini scones for about 12 minutes, or until golden. Before serving, sprinkle lightly with icing sugar. Serve with jam and Quick Crème Fraîche (page 119) or any flavoured butter.

Variations

Apricot, Candied Ginger & Raw Sugar Scones

Make scone base, omitting the lemon zest and white chocolate chips. Add instead ½ cup chopped dried apricots and ¼ cup chopped candied ginger. Sprinkle with raw sugar. Sprinkle lightly with icing sugar before serving.

Parmesan Cheese, Cheddar Cheese & Green Onion Scones

Make scone base, omitting sugar, lemon zest and white chocolate chips. Blend in ½ cup grated Parmesan cheese, ½ cup grated cheddar cheese and 3 tablespoons chopped green onion or chives. Once scones are formed, garnish with ¼ cup Parmesan cheese and sprinkle with coarse salt, for example, fleur de sel.

Breakfast Crescents

14 ounces	frozen puff pastry, thawed
1	egg, beaten with 1 teaspoon cold water
½ cup	chocolate hazelnut spread or Nutella
	icing sugar to garnish

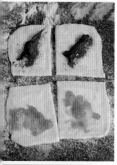

Preheat oven to 400°F. Lightly grease a baking sheet or line with parchment paper.

Roll out the puff pastry on a lightly floured surface. Form 4 square pieces, $^1\!/_{16}$-inch thick. Paint the edges of each square with the beaten-egg wash.

Divide the chocolate hazelnut spread into 4 portions. Put one portion in the middle of each square. Roll the square starting with a corner.

Place on baking trays with the tips tucked under and the ends slightly curved in to form a crescent shape. Brush crescents with the beaten-egg wash. Bake in oven for about 20 minutes or until golden brown.

Garnish with sifted icing sugar.

Serve warm.

These crescents take only 15 minutes prep time. Great for all ages!

Variation

Omit the chocolate hazelnut spread and instead add about ½ cup of apricot jam or any fruit jam.

Ricotta Lime Muffins

MAKES 8 LARGE MUFFINS

1 cup	all-purpose flour
2 teaspoons	baking powder
⅓ cup	butter, softened
½ cup	sugar
1 cup	ricotta
2	limes (zest and juice)
2	eggs, lightly beaten

For glaze

1	lime (zest and juice)
¼ cup	sugar

Preheat oven to 350°F. Grease muffin tins or line tins with 4- x 4-inch parchment paper squares.

In a bowl, sift together flour and baking powder.

In another bowl, cream together butter and sugar. Add ricotta and zest and juice of 2 limes. Stir in beaten eggs. Fold wet ingredients into flour mixture.

Fill the muffin tins with the muffin batter and bake for 20–25 minutes.

For the glaze, whisk together the zest and juice of 1 lime and the sugar. While muffins are still warm drizzle with the glaze.

This is a fabulous summer muffin – serve with fresh fruit or Blueberry Lime Jam (page 124).

Chocolate-Surprise Muffins

MAKES 12 MEDIUM MUFFINS OR 18 MINI MUFFINS

These chocolate muffins are also fabulous without jam or cream cheese. For fun and a different look and taste, substitute white chocolate chips.

2 cups	semisweet chocolate chips
⅓ cup	butter
1	egg, beaten
¼ cup	brown sugar
¾ cup	buttermilk
1 tablespoon	pure vanilla
2 cups	all-purpose flour
1 teaspoon	baking soda
⅓ cup	raspberry jam or other jam
½ cup	cream cheese

Preheat oven to 350°F. Grease muffin tins.

In a double boiler, melt 1 cup chocolate chips with butter over low heat, or melt in a microwave for about 1 minute.

In a large bowl, combine the chocolate mixture, beaten egg, brown sugar, buttermilk and pure vanilla. Fold in flour and baking soda, then the remaining 1 cup chocolate chips. Scoop mixture into prepared muffin tins so cups are half full. Spoon 1 teaspoon of jam and cream cheese each into the middle of the batter of each muffin. Top with remaining batter so muffin tins are three-quarters full. (Do not overfill.)

Bake medium muffins for approximately 25 minutes and mini muffins for about 20 minutes. Leave muffins to cool in tins for 10 minutes.

Delicious when served still warm. I serve mini Chocolate-Surprise Muffins at dinner parties as an easy but decadent dessert.

Gingerbread Muffins with Cream Cheese Icing

MAKES 12 LARGE MUFFINS

Instead of cream cheese icing, place a teaspoon of cream cheese in the centre of each muffin when filling the tins, and bake.

2¼ cups	all-purpose flour
2 teaspoons	baking powder
1 teaspoon	baking soda
½ teaspoon	salt
2 teaspoons	cinnamon
2 teaspoons	ginger
½ teaspoon	allspice
½ cup	butter, softened
½ cup	brown sugar
¼ cup	fancy molasses
2	eggs
¾ cup	yoghurt, vanilla or plain; or buttermilk
2 cups	shredded carrots or peeled and grated apple
¼ cup	cream cheese
1 tablespoon	butter, softened
1 cup	icing sugar, sifted
1 teaspoon	pure vanilla
1 tablespoon	white chocolate chips, melted and cooled
½ teaspoon	lemon zest
	cinnamon for garnish

Preheat oven to 350°F.

To make the muffins, whisk together flour, baking powder, baking soda, salt, cinnamon, ginger and allspice in a large bowl.

In a separate bowl, beat the butter with brown sugar until light and fluffy. Add the molasses and then the eggs one at a time.

Fold the flour mixture into the butter mixture, alternating with the yoghurt. Fold in the carrots.

Spoon the batter into 12 greased muffin tins. Bake about 20 minutes or until tester comes out clean. Allow muffins to cool in tins for 5 minutes, then transfer onto racks.

To make the icing, cream together cream cheese and butter. Mix in icing sugar, vanilla, white chocolate chips and zest. When the muffins are completely cool, frost with the cream cheese icing. Lightly sprinkle the iced muffins with cinnamon overtop.

Raspberry Bran Muffins

MAKES 12 MEDIUM MUFFINS

2 cups	all-purpose flour
1½ cups	wheat bran
½ cup	brown sugar
4 teaspoons	baking powder
½ teaspoon	salt
1 tablespoon	cinnamon
½ cup	vegetable oil
2	eggs, beaten
1½ cups	buttermilk or yoghurt
1 teaspoon	pure vanilla
¾ cup	pecans, chopped
1½ cups	raspberries, fresh or frozen
	raw sugar for garnish

Blueberries, loganberries or blackberries may be substituted for the raspberries.

Preheat oven to 350°F. Grease muffin tins.

Combine the flour, wheat bran, brown sugar, baking powder, salt and cinnamon in a large bowl.

In a separate bowl, whisk together vegetable oil, eggs, buttermilk and pure vanilla. Fold liquid ingredients into dry ingredients and add pecans. Do not overmix. Divide half the batter between the prepared muffin tins. Place 3–4 raspberries in each muffin cup and top with the remaining batter. Sprinkle with raw sugar. Bake for 20–25 minutes.

Allow muffins to cool for 5 minutes before removing from muffin tins.

Fantastic when served still warm. This is a very light bran muffin, and not too sweet.

Special Occasion Breakfast

Fairholme Maple-Pecan Granola,
served with Greek yoghurt with honey and fresh fruit

Ricotta Lime Muffins,
served with Blueberry Lime Jam
or
Lemon White-Chocolate Raw Sugar Scone,
served with Quick Crème Fraîche
or
Breakfast Crescents

Herb & Cheddar Scrambled Egg Strudel, served
with roasted asparagus and Pan-Roasted Cherry Tomatoes
or
Individual Baby Potato, Cheese, Bacon & Thyme Frittatas,
served with Chive & Black Pepper Popovers
or
Overnight Belgian Waffles with Hazelnuts,
served with Strawberry Syrup and whipping cream

Freshly squeezed orange juice
or
Gingery Snicket

Coffee or tea

Special Occasion Brunch

Maple Scones,
served with Pumpkin Spice Spread
or
Parmesan Cheese, Cheddar Cheese & Green Onion Scones

Roasted Vegetable & Three-Cheese Frittata,
served with Parmesan Cheese Sautéed Potatoes
and smoked salmon or back bacon
or
Raspberry Upside-Down Buttermilk Pancakes,
with white chocolate chips, fresh raspberries
and maple syrup

Sautéed Lemon and Herb Prawns,
served with Caesar Salad
or
Crab Cakes with Lemon Crème Fraîche,
served with fresh baby greens and Lemony Italian Dressing

Overnight Pecan Coffee Cake
or
Chocolate Tuxedo Strawberries

Italian or French 75

Coffee or tea

Special Occasion Lunch

Butternut Squash & Coconut Milk Soup,
served with Double-Cheese Muffins
or
Easy Vegetable Soup,
served with Sprouted Grain Bread
and Italian Cream Cheese Spread

Caprese Salad
or
Curried Chicken Lettuce Cups

Spinach Ricotta Cups,
served with Pan-Roasted Cherry Tomatoes
or
Fresh Basil Tomato Sauce & Spaghettini
or
Creamy Crimini Mushroom Phyllo Cups

Viennese Apple Strudel
or
Espresso Chocolate Loaf

Nabokov's Pear
Sparkling mineral water with lemon or lime

Coffee or tea

French or Italian 75

MAKES 1 COCKTAIL

¼ ounce	Cointreau (triple sec)
¼ ounce	Tanqueray (gin)
	juice of ¼ lemon
	champagne for the French version
	rosé Prosecco for the Italian version

Put all 3 ingredients into a martini shaker. Shake and strain into champagne flute. Top with champagne or Prosecco. Garnish with a twist of lemon.

Crisp, citrusy and refreshing. Commonly drank as an aperitif, the 75 pairs well with a plate of raw oysters.

Nabokov's Pear

MAKES 1 COCKTAIL

1½ ounces	Stoli Vanil (Stolichnaya vanilla vodka)
½ ounce	peach schnapps
3 ounces	pear nectar
	mandarin slice (very thin slice) of pear

Place the sliced pear against the inside of the chilled glass near the rim. If the pear is sliced thin enough, it should stick. Pour vodka, schnapps and pear nectar into a shaker full of ice. Shake vigorously and strain into a martini glass (carefully, as to not dislodge the garnish). Serve.

The Nabokov is simple and dangerously easy to drink. I find unfiltered pear nectars work best here. If you can see the "sand" at the bottom of your finished drink, you know you've got it right.

Gingery Snicket

1 ounce	fresh squeezed lemon juice
1 ounce	sugar syrup (1 part sugar and 1 part water, boiled to dissolve)
3 dashes	grapefruit bitters
	ginger ale
	grapefruit segment, skin removed

Pour the lemon juice and sugar syrup over ice in a glass tumbler. Add bitters and stir. Top with ginger ale and float the grapefruit segment over ice. Serve.

The Snicket was a virgin cocktail born of necessity as a non-alcoholic alternative for expecting mothers, designated drivers and other sober folk. However, after the baby is born and the car is home, an ounce of gin will find itself in good company here.

Chicken Salad Niçoise

For the salad

4 cups	chicken stock
4	chicken breasts, boneless and skinless
1 cup	green beans, blanched and sliced lengthwise
4 cups	baby salad greens
⅓ cup	kalamata olives
12	cherry tomatoes, halved (red and/or yellow)
4	eggs, hard boiled, peeled and halved
1 tablespoon	capers, drained

Smoked tuna can be substituted for the chicken. So easy because it doesn't need to be cooked.

For the dressing

2 cloves	garlic, minced
1 tablespoon	lemon juice or red wine vinegar
2 teaspoons	grainy mustard
⅓ cup	extra virgin olive oil
dash	salt
dash	pepper

To make the salad, in a saucepan bring the chicken stock to boil. Reduce heat to medium-low, add the chicken breasts and cook for about 20 minutes. Drain off the chicken stock (you can reserve or freeze for another use). Cool chicken breasts in refrigerator and slice just before serving.

Blanch the green beans in salted, boiling water for about 2–4 minutes, depending on thickness. Plunge in cold water, then drain and dry on a clean cloth or paper towel.

To make the dressing, whisk together the garlic, lemon juice, mustard, oil, salt and pepper. Set aside.

Plate the salad with salad greens, cooked chicken, blanched green beans, olives and cherry tomatoes. Top with eggs and capers. Cover lightly with the dressing.

Serve with Sprouted Grain Bread (page 46) and butter for a great lunch!

Caprese Salad

SERVES 4

4	large heirloom or Roma tomatoes
12	cherry tomatoes, halved
dash	salt
dash	pepper
¼ cup	fresh basil leaves, torn
4	medium buffalo mozzarella balls, fresh mozzarella balls or Burrata cheese balls
¼ cup	extra virgin olive oil
1–2 tablespoons	balsamic vinegar
	additional basil leaves for garnish
¼ cup	kalamata olives for garnish

During tomato season take advantage of local farmers' markets for a variety of heirloom tomatoes in various colours and shapes.

Cut tomatoes into wedges or rounds and place onto serving plate. Add cherry tomatoes. Sprinkle with salt and pepper. Add basil and a mozzarella ball on each plate. Drizzle with olive oil and balsamic vinegar. Garnish with basil leaves and olives.

Serve with crusty baguette, focaccia bread or Sprouted Grain Bread (page 46).

On a trip to Venice I had Burrata cheese instead of buffalo mozzarella. It was so delicious. Burrata cheese is similar to a fresh mozzarella, but creamier and richer. Burrata cheese is usually available in Italian or specialty delicatessens.

Caesar Salad

SERVES 4–6

For the croutons

2 tablespoons	butter, melted
2 tablespoons	extra virgin olive oil
4 thick slices	white or focaccia bread, cut into 1-inch cubes
dash	salt
dash	pepper
dash	cayenne

For the salad

2–3 cloves	garlic, minced
2–4	anchovy fillets, mashed
½ teaspoon	salt
2 tablespoons	lemon juice, freshly squeezed
dash	pepper
½ teaspoon	Worcestershire sauce
½ teaspoon	Tabasco sauce
1 teaspoon	Dijon mustard
2 teaspoons	capers, minced
1	egg yolk
½ cup	extra virgin olive oil
1 large head	Romaine lettuce (washed and dried)
1 cup	Parmesan cheese, grated, plus a bit of extra cheese for garnish

To make the croutons, preheat oven to 450°F.

Combine butter and oil in a bowl. Add the cubed bread and mix until coated. Season with salt, pepper and cayenne then mix again. Spread seasoned bread cubes onto baking sheet. Bake for about 10 minutes until croutons are golden.

To make the salad, place garlic, anchovy fillets and salt in a large bowl. With a fork, mash into a paste. Add the lemon juice, pepper, Worcestershire sauce, Tabasco sauce, Dijon mustard, capers and egg yolk. Using a whisk, slowly add the oil. Add Romaine lettuce and Parmesan cheese and toss.

Top with croutons and a bit of grated Parmesan cheese. Serve immediately.

Honey-Dijon Vinaigrette

MAKES ¾ CUP

¼ cup	sherry vinegar or red wine vinegar
1 tablespoon	lemon juice
1 tablespoon	honey or maple syrup
1 tablespoon	Dijon mustard
1 teaspoon	garlic, minced
⅓ cup	olive oil
½ teaspoon	salt
dash	pepper

Whisk together the vinegar, lemon juice, honey, mustard and garlic. Keep whisking and gradually add the oil, salt and pepper.

To keep the greens well shaped, pack a 2-cup plastic container with the greens and place carefully onto plate. Drizzle 1 tablespoon of dressing over greens.

Garnish with edible flowers or fresh herbs.

Lemony Italian Dressing

MAKES ⅓ CUP

zest	1 lemon
2 tablespoons	fresh lemon juice
1 teaspoon	sugar
dash	salt
dash	pepper
¼ cup	olive oil or a mixture of olive oil and grapeseed oil

Combine lemon zest, juice, sugar, salt and pepper. Gradually whisk in oil.

Delicious with fresh baby greens or baby spinach. Add a tablespoon of chopped fresh mint to give your salad a fresh taste.

Curried Chicken Lettuce Cups

SERVES 4

2 cups	chicken, skinless, cooked and chopped
½ cup	mayonnaise
½ cup	sour cream or plain yoghurt
¼ cup	parsley, chopped
dash	Tabasco sauce
dash	hot chili flakes
dash	salt
dash	black pepper
1 tablespoon	curry powder
4 tablespoons	lemon juice
2 large	shallots, chopped and sautéed in 1 tablespoon butter
8 large	lettuce leaves (butter lettuce, iceberg, escarole, endive)
½ cup	almonds, sliced and toasted

For the giant croutons, slice 4 diagonal ¼-inch slices from a baguette. Brush bread with about 2 tablespoons olive oil and bake at 350°F for about 15–20 minutes or until golden.

Mix together all ingredients except lettuce and almonds.

Fill individual lettuce leaves with chicken filling. Sprinkle with toasted almonds.

Serve with Sprouted Grain Bread (page 46), a giant crouton, or with one of Fairholme's soups. The curried chicken can also be used as a sandwich filling.

This recipe will double or triple easily. This makes a great brunch or lunch dish served with a crisp salad and simple Lemony Italian Dressing (page 87).

Variation

Substitute shrimp or turkey for the chicken.

Easy French Onion Soup

SERVES 4

1 tablespoon	olive oil
2 large	onions, sliced
2	leeks, white part only, thinly sliced
1 teaspoon	sugar
3 cloves	garlic, chopped
½ cup	dry white wine
6 cups	stock (beef or vegetable)
1	bay leaf
1 teaspoon	fresh thyme, chopped
1 teaspoon	salt
½ teaspoon	pepper
4 slices	baguette, sliced ¼-inch thick
¾ cup	white cheddar cheese or Gruyere, grated

Heat oil in a saucepan over medium heat. Sauté the onions and leeks until translucent, about 10 minutes.

Add the sugar and continue to cook over low heat until the mixture is caramelized, about 20 minutes. Adding sugar speeds the caramelization process.

Add the garlic, wine, stock and bay leaf and cook another 20 minutes approximately. Season the soup with thyme, salt and pepper. Take out bay leaf.

Preheat the broiler in oven. Spoon the soup into 4 ovenproof bowls. Place one slice baguette on top of soup in each bowl and top with the cheese.

Place bowls in oven under the broiler and broil until the cheese becomes golden brown, about 3–5 minutes.

Delicious served with a crisp green salad drizzled with our Honey-Dijon Vinaigrette (page 87).

Easy Vegetable Soup

SERVES 4–6

2 tablespoons	olive oil
1	medium onion, finely chopped
2 cloves	garlic, minced
4 cups	fresh or canned tomatoes, diced or crushed
4 cups	stock (chicken or vegetable)
2	celery stalks, chopped
2	carrots, peeled and chopped
2	small zucchinis, peeled and chopped
1	red pepper, chopped
2 teaspoons	fresh thyme, finely chopped
6–8	fresh basil leaves, torn
dash	salt
dash	pepper
½ cup	Parmesan cheese, grated to serve
	extra basil leaves for garnish

In a large saucepan, heat oil over medium heat and sauté the onion and garlic until translucent, about 5 minutes. Be careful not to burn the garlic. Add tomatoes, stock, celery, carrots, zucchini, red pepper and thyme.

Cover and bring to boil, then reduce heat to simmer and cook for another 15–20 minutes until vegetables are tender. Add basil leaves and season with salt, pepper and Parmesan cheese. Garnish soup with extra basil leaves.

Serve with Sprouted Grain Bread (page 46) or Double-Cheese Muffins (page 52).

Butternut Squash & Coconut Milk Soup

SERVES 4

2 tablespoons	butter
1 tablespoon	olive oil
1 cup	onion, coarsely chopped
1 cup	leeks, white part only, chopped
3 pounds	butternut squash, peeled, seeded and cubed
3 cups	stock (chicken or vegetable)
1–2 teaspoons	salt
dash	pepper
1 cup	coconut milk
2 teaspoons	cilantro, chopped, to garnish (optional)

In a large saucepan, heat the butter and oil over medium heat. Sauté onion and leeks for about 10 minutes. Add the cubed squash, stock, salt and pepper.

Cover and simmer for about 20 minutes over medium-low heat until the squash is tender. In a blender, blend the soup for about 1 minute until smooth.

Return to the pot, add the coconut milk and heat to serve.

Garnish with cilantro and serve with bread and butter.

Also superb when made with other winter squashes, such as buttercup squash.

Fresh Spinach Soup

SERVES 4

1 large	russet or Yukon Gold potato, peeled and cubed
2 cloves	garlic, coarsely chopped
2 tablespoons	olive oil
6 ounces	baby spinach
2 cups	stock (chicken or vegetable)
½ cup	light cream, plain yoghurt or Quick Crème Fraîche (page 119) (optional)
2 tablespoons	flat-leaf parsley, chopped
dash	salt
dash	pepper

Boil potato in salted water until tender.

In a large skillet, sauté garlic in oil over low heat until translucent. Add spinach to skillet and cook over low heat for about 5 minutes.

In a blender add the stock, boiled potato and spinach mixture. Blend for about 1 minute until smooth.

Ladle into individual serving bowls. Add cream and sprinkle with parsley. Season with salt and pepper before serving.

Crab Cakes with Lemon Crème Fraîche

SERVES 4

2 small	leeks, whites only, finely sliced
1 tablespoon	butter
2 cups	crab meat, cooked
½ cup	mayonnaise
3	egg yolks, lightly beaten
2	green onions, chopped
½ teaspoon	cayenne
dash	salt
dash	pepper
2 cups	fresh breadcrumbs
¼ cup	vegetable oil (for frying)
1 recipe	Lemon Crème Fraîche (page 119)

Salsas are also a great addition to this delicious dish.

Prepare the Lemon Crème Frâiche.

In a skillet, sauté leeks in butter until tender. Set aside.

In a bowl, combine crab, sauteéd leeks, mayonnaise, egg yolks, green onions, cayenne, salt and pepper. Mix well and add ½ cup of the breadcrumbs and mix again. Place the remaining 1½ cups breadcrumbs on a plate.

Line a baking sheet with plastic wrap.

Form crab mixture into 8 cakes. Coat each cake with breadcrumbs and place on parchment-lined baking sheet. Chill in refrigerator until firm, about 1 hour.

In a non-stick skillet, heat vegetable oil over medium heat. Fry crab cakes, turning once until golden brown, about 4 minutes per side. Place on paper towel to drain excess oil.

Serve immediately with 2–3 tablespoons Lemon Crème Fraîche per serving.

Lemon & Herb Prawns

SERVES 4

1 pound	prawns, peeled
2 tablespoons	olive oil
1 teaspoon	garlic, minced
¼ cup	mixed fresh herbs, chopped
	(e.g., flat-leaf parsley, tarragon or basil)
1 tablespoon	lemon zest
1 tablespoon	lemon juice
dash	salt
dash	pepper

In a large skillet, sauté prawns in olive oil over medium heat for about 3 minutes. Add remaining ingredients and continue cooking for another 3 minutes.

Serve with fresh mixed greens dressed with Lemony Italian Dressing (page 87).

Fresh Basil Tomato Sauce & Spaghettini

SERVES 4

This sauce can be cooked without the basil several hours in advance and then reheated to serve.

For the sauce

3 cloves	garlic, minced
⅓ cup	extra virgin olive oil
3 cups	Roma tomatoes, fresh or canned
dash	salt
dash	pepper
12	fresh basil leaves, torn into pieces
	additional basil for garnish
	Parmesan cheese, grated

For the pasta

1 pound	dried spaghettini or spaghetti

To make the sauce, sauté garlic in oil in a large saucepan over medium heat until translucent, about 3–5 minutes. Add tomatoes and reduce heat. Simmer uncovered for about 20 minutes. Add salt and pepper.

To preserve the flavour and colour of the basil leaves, add them to sauce just before serving.

To make the pasta, bring 8 cups of cold, salted water in a large pot to a boil. Add spaghettini and cook until al dente, about 8 minutes. Drain.

In a large bowl, toss the hot pasta with the basil tomato sauce. Add freshly grated Parmesan cheese, top with additional basil and serve immediately.

Make sure to use a good quality Parmesan cheese for this dish.

This pasta sauce is very popular at my house – easy to make but so delicious!

Fairholme Basil Pesto

MAKES 1½ CUPS

For extra cheese flavour, use 4 tablespoons of Pecorino Romano cheese with the Parmesan.

½ cup	pine nuts
½ cup	Parmesan or Pecorino Romano cheese, grated
1 tablespoon	flat-leaf parsley, chopped
2 cups	fresh basil leaves, packed down
3 cloves	garlic
¾ cup	extra virgin olive oil
	salt and pepper to taste

In a food processor equipped with a chopping blade, pulse pine nuts, cheese, parsley, basil and garlic. Then chop on full power to mince. Turn power back down and slowly stream in oil so that the pesto becomes mayonnaise-like in consistency. (This is key to a good pesto.) Add salt and pepper.

Keep in refrigerator for up to 10 days, or freeze up to 3 months in ice-cube trays.

Use 1–2 tablespoons of pesto per person for a pasta serving. Also use for pesto bruschetta. Just spread pesto over sliced, chargrilled or toasted Italian bread or baguette.

Middle Eastern Houmous

SERVES 4–6

juice	2 large lemons
2 cups	canned chickpeas, drained and rinsed
2 tablespoons	tahini
3 cloves	garlic, crushed
3–4 tablespoons	water
¼ cup	olive oil
dash	paprika
dash	cumin
	extra chickpeas
	pita bread

In a blender, add lemon juice, chickpeas, tahini, garlic and water. Pulse to create a creamy consistency.

Place houmous in the centre of a serving dish and spread out, leaving a 2-inch border. While turning plate, with the back of a spoon form a moat in the houmous near the border of the plate. Drizzle olive oil into the moat. Sprinkle with paprika and cumin and add a few chickpeas on border of plate to garnish.

Serve with pita bread.

This houmous is so quick to make – it's a favourite at my house!

Variation

For *baba ghanouj*, use peeled and roasted eggplants instead of the chickpeas and follow the same process.

Fresh from Restaurant Nora

Nora Pouillon is a pioneer and champion of organic, environmentally conscious cuisine. Born in Vienna, Austria, Nora came to Washington, D.C., in the late 1960s. She was shocked to discover the processed, chemical-laden foods Americans were eating, which she realized contributed to their health problems. That's when she embarked on her crusade to promote a healthier lifestyle.

In the 1970s, Nora began to develop an extensive network of organic and natural farmers, personally driving out to farms in the Washington, D.C., area to purchase local produce and meats for her family and her cooking class/catering business. When she opened Restaurant Nora in 1979, she continued to use these farmers to supply the restaurant with seasonal organic produce while introducing other D.C. chefs to the farmers as well. She also initiated D.C.'s first producer-only farmer's market, called FRESHFARM Markets, which now includes 11 markets in the metropolitan area.

By the mid-1990s, nearly all of the products used at Restaurant Nora were certified organic. Nora sought out Oregon Tilth, a certifying agency, and worked with them for two years to establish the organic certification standards for restaurants. In 1999, Restaurant Nora became the first certified organic restaurant in the United States, a feat accomplished by few since.

Nora tirelessly advocates her commitment to nutritionally wholesome food and a sustainable, health-focused lifestyle based on the premise that you are what you eat, drink and breathe. This philosophy not only extends to her restaurant, which will celebrate its 34th year in business in 2012, but also to her outreach work. Each year, Nora hosts five interns from the organization Women Chefs & Restaurateurs at the restaurant, and she sits on the board of directors of seven food and environmental organizations. Nora is the author of *Cooking with Nora*, a seasonal menu cookbook that was a finalist for the Julia Child Cookbook Award, and she is currently working on her memoirs.

I am excited to have Nora, who is my cousin, be part of this book. The photo at left is by Matthew Rakola.

Low-Fat Guacamole

1 cup	avocado, peeled and seeded
¾ cup	fresh or frozen green peas (defrosted)
1 tablespoon	lime or lemon juice
¼ teaspoon	cumin
½ teaspoon	salt
¼ teaspoon	pepper
2 tablespoons	cilantro, chopped
1 or less	chili pepper, chopped
⅛ teaspoon	cayenne pepper, optional
1 tablespoon	scallions, chopped
1 teaspoon	garlic, minced
½ cup	water
1 teaspoon	grated lime or lemon rind

Purée all ingredients together in blender or food processor until smooth. Taste for seasoning.

Great to serve as a relish or with any kind of grilled seafood, such as shrimp, calamari, scallops, salmon or halibut. It is also good with fresh crab meat.

Mushroom, Ham & Spinach Bruschetta

SERVES 4

4 slices	country bread, sliced ¾-inch thick
1 clove	garlic, peeled
4 teaspoons	olive oil
3 tablespoons	shallots, minced
1 teaspoon	garlic, minced
½ pound	chanterelle, crimini or other mushrooms, wiped clean or briefly washed, drained and dried (if the mushrooms are large, slice them thickly)
1 teaspoon	dry sherry wine or sherry vinegar
2 ounces	baby spinach or arugula, washed and stemmed
4–6 ounces	smoked ham, cut in julienne or matchlike strips
	sea salt and freshly ground black pepper to taste
2 tablespoons	chopped parsley for garnish

Make the bruschetta by toasting or grilling the bread until crusty and firm. Rub the bread generously on one side with the garlic clove.

Heat the olive oil in a medium pan. Add the shallots and garlic and sauté for about 1 minute. Be careful not to burn the garlic. Add the mushrooms and sauté on medium high heat for about 5 minutes or until the mushrooms are cooked. Add the sherry and cook over high heat for 1 minute to reduce. Add the spinach and the ham. Sauté and stir until the greens are slightly wilted and the ham is warmed through.

Season with the salt and pepper, being careful with the salt as cured meat is often quite salty.

To assemble, put each bruschetta on a warmed dinner-size plate. Spoon the mushroom mixture on top of the bruschetta. Garnish with the parsley and the juices from the sauté pan.

The photo above of fresh chanterelle mushrooms was taken early in the morning in the Rialto Market in Venice, Italy, by my daughter Simone.

Smoked Salmon & Asparagus Pasta

1 pound	pasta (any tubular pasta will do)
2 tablespoons	butter
2 tablespoons	olive oil
1 small	red onion, thinly sliced
1 bunch	thin asparagus, cut diagonally into 1-inch pieces
4–8 ounces	smoked salmon, cut into 1- to 2-inch strips
1 tablespoon	fresh dill or parsley, chopped
	salt and ground pepper to taste

Cook the pasta in plenty of salted water until al dente. Drain and return to pot.

Melt butter and heat oil in a pan, and sauté onions until translucent. Add the asparagus and stir-fry until cooked but still crisp. Toss mixture with pasta in the pot and add smoked salmon and dill. Taste for seasoning before serving.

For a festive touch, add a dollop of Quick Crème Fraîche (page 119) and some black caviar.

Smoked Trout & Crispy Potato with Apple Horseradish Sauce

SERVES 4

For the potato fries

2 large	potatoes, peeled and cut to the size of French fries
3 tablespoons	olive oil
	sea salt and pepper to taste

For the sauce

4 tablespoons	freshly grated horseradish or 2 tablespoons drained prepared horseradish
¼ cup	low-fat yogurt drained for at least ½ an hour in a cheesecloth or coffee filter, or ¼ cup sour cream
1 tablespoon	lemon juice
1	apple, peeled and grated
	sea salt and pepper to taste
4 pieces	smoked trout, sturgeon, salmon, tuna or halibut filet, skinned and boned
½ cup	fresh mâche lettuce or watercress

To make the crispy fries, toss potatoes in a bowl with olive oil and salt and pepper.

Place on a cookie sheet and bake in a 375°F oven for about 20 minutes, until golden brown and cooked. Remove and drain on paper towels.

To make the sauce, combine all the sauce ingredients and mix well.

Divide the potatoes onto 4 plates and arrange attractively. Place smoked fish on top of the fries, and serve with a dollop of the apple horseradish sauce. Garnish with lettuce or watercress.

Strawberry Syrup

1–2 tablespoon	water
¼ cup	sugar
1 tablespoon	fresh lemon juice
1 teaspoon	lemon zest
2 cups	strawberries, fresh or frozen

In a saucepan, simmer water, sugar, lemon juice and lemon zest over medium heat until sugar is dissolved. Add strawberries and cook for a few minutes until liquid is reduced and a sauce-like consistency is reached. Pour mixture into a blender. Blend until you have a smooth purée.

Great with Overnight Belgian Waffles with Hazelnuts (page 33), Ricotta Blintzes (page 34) or even as a dip for the Espresso Chocolate Loaf (page 135).

Warm Bumbleberry Coulis

MAKES 1½ CUPS

½ cup	raspberries
½ cup	blueberries
½ cup	blackberries
¼ cup	sugar
1 tablespoon	fresh lemon juice

In a saucepan simmer berries, sugar and lemon juice over medium heat. Cook until berries are soft, about 10 minutes. Pour mixture into blender. Blend until you have a smooth purée.

Serve with Overnight Belgian Waffles with Hazelnuts (page 33), Ricotta Blintzes with Strawberry Syrup (page 34) or even as a dip for the Espresso Chocolate Loaf (page 135).

Quick Crème Fraîche

MAKES 2 CUPS

1 cup	sour cream
1 cup	whipping cream

Mix together sour cream and whipping cream.

Loosely cover and let stand at room temperature for 16 hours. Then refrigerate until mixture has thickened, generally overnight.

Lemon Crème Fraîche

MAKES 2 CUPS

1 cup	sour cream
1 cup	whipping cream
zest	1 lemon

Mix together the whipping cream and sour cream.

Let stand at room temperature loosely covered for about 16 hours. Then refrigerate until mixture has thickened, generally overnight. Stir in lemon zest.

Chipotle Ketchup

MAKES 1 CUP

1 cup	ketchup
1½ teaspoons	chipotle, chopped
2 tablespoons	adobo sauce
1 tablespoon	balsamic or sherry vinegar

Combine all the ingredients together and store in the fridge as you would store-bought ketchup.

Serve with Baked Eggs in Ham Cups (page 20) and Parmesan Cheese Sautéed Potatoes (page 12). A great way to spice up an egg dish.

Italian Cream Cheese Spread

1 cup	cream cheese
1 tablespoon	olive oil
2 teaspoons	balsamic vinegar or red wine vinegar
2 cloves	garlic, crushed
1 teaspoon	chili peppers, without seeds
¼ teaspoon	salt

Combine all the ingredients in a bowl.

This cream cheese dip is so simple to make, but is always a hit. Serve with Sprouted Grain Bread (page 46) or crackers.

Orange or Lemon Butter

MAKES 1 CUP

1 cup	butter, softened
1 teaspoon	orange or lemon zest, grated
¼ cup	powdered sugar

In food processor or with a mixer, whip together all the ingredients. Blend together for about a minute until light and fluffy. Cover and refrigerate until ready to serve.

Great with scones, pancakes or waffles.

Herb Lemon Butter

MAKES 1 CUP

1 cup	butter, softened
1 teaspoon	lemon zest
¼ cup	chives, tarragon, basil or flat-leaf parsley, finely chopped
dash	salt

In food processor or with a mixer, whip together all ingredients and blend until combined.

Place parchment or plastic wrap on a work surface. Spoon blended butter onto the parchment, placing on the edge closest to you. Fold parchment over the butter and roll into a log, twisting the ends. Roll the butter tightly to avoid air bubbles.

Refrigerate rolled butter until solid. Herb butter can be stored in refrigerator up to 2 weeks or frozen for up to 3 months.

Serve with any breads and grilled fish or meats.

Flavoured butters freeze very well, up to 3 months. For parties, hosts can roll out the butter between 2 pieces of plastic wrap, chill, then punch out butter shapes with cookie cutters and serve.

Cranberry Butter

MAKES 2 CUPS

2 cups	cranberries, fresh or frozen
¼ cup	orange juice
1 teaspoon	orange zest
¼ cup	sugar
1 cup	butter at room temperature

In a small saucepan over medium-high heat, combine all the ingredients except butter. Bring to a boil, then turn down heat to medium-low. Cook for about 15–20 minutes until syrupy. Remove from heat and let cool.

In a food processor, blend the butter and cranberry mixture for a few minutes. Cover and refrigerate until ready to serve.

Garnish with a cherry or other fruit for a sweet and simple look.

Honey Butter

MAKES 1 CUP

1 cup	butter, softened
4 tablespoons	honey
½ teaspoon	cinnamon

In a mixer, beat all the ingredients for about a minute until light and fluffy.

Serve at room temperature with toast or scones.

If you'd like to make a warm Honey Butter, heat all ingredients in a small saucepan over low heat until melted. Serve with waffles, pancakes or French toast.

Blueberry Lime Jam

The lime adds such a great flavour to this yummy jam.

4½ cups	blueberries, fresh or frozen
5 cups	sugar
1 tablespoon	lime zest
⅓ cup	fresh lime juice
1½ packages	pectin powder (use 2 packages of pectin for frozen berries)

Wash and then crush blueberries in a blender.

In large, heavy-bottomed pot, add blueberries, sugar, zest and lime juice. Bring to a boil over high heat, stirring constantly. Boil for 1 minute.

Remove from heat and stir in pectin. Stir jam for 5 minutes while skimming off foam. Pour jam into sterilized jars, seal and store in refrigerator.

Bumbleberry Jam

5 cups	mixed berries, fresh or frozen (e.g., raspberries, strawberries, blackberries or loganberries)
7 cups	sugar
1 teaspoon	vanilla or 1 vanilla bean, cut in half and scraped
1½ packages	pectin powder (use 2 packages of pectin for frozen berries)

Wash berries and then crush with potato masher.

In large, heavy-bottomed pot, add berries, sugar and vanilla. Bring to a boil over high heat, stirring constantly. Boil for 1 minute.

Remove from heat and stir in pectin. Stir jam for 5 minutes while skimming off foam. (If using vanilla bean, remove and discard.) Pour jam into sterilized jars, seal and store in refrigerator.

This jam is a favourite with our guests. Delicious with scones, muffins or Sprouted Grain Bread (page 46).

Lemon-Orange Curd

MAKES 1 CUP

4 tablespoons	butter
½ cup	lemon juice
¼ cup	orange juice
1 cup	sugar
4	eggs
2	egg yolks
zest	1 lemon
zest	½ orange

In a saucepan, whisk together butter and lemon and orange juice and bring to a boil.

In a bowl, whisk together sugar, eggs and yolks. Put the mixture through a sieve to prevent egg-white clumps from forming.

While stirring, slowly add the egg mixture to the hot juice mixture in the saucepan until combined. Cook for about 10 minutes, stirring constantly. When curd thickens, remove from heat and stir in the lemon and orange zests.

Serve warm or cold. Perfect with Cranberry Walnut Scones (page 55).

Pumpkin Spice Spread

MAKES 1 CUP

2 tablespoons	packed dark brown sugar
1 tablespoon	maple syrup
1 tablespoon	water
dash	allspice
dash	ginger
dash	cloves
dash	nutmeg
½ teaspoon	cinnamon
¾ cup	canned pumpkin purée

Mix all ingredients in a saucepan. Bring to a boil, then reduce heat to a simmer. Simmer for about 15–20 minutes, stirring constantly until mixture thickens.

Serve warm or cold. Delicious with our Maple Scones (page 56), Overnight Belgian Waffles with Hazelnuts (page 33) or just on plain toast in place of butter.

Chocolate Tuxedo Strawberries

MAKES 1 DOZEN CHOCOLATE STRAWBERRIES

12 large	strawberries with stems on, washed and dried very well
1 cup	dark chocolate, chopped
1 cup	milk or white chocolate, chopped

For best results use quality chocolate. Do not overheat the chocolate while melting or it will lose its shine when it cools.

Be sure to dry the strawberries well and make sure no water gets into the melted chocolate.

Line a baking sheet with parchment paper.

Melt the dark chocolate in a medium bowl in a double boiler. Cool chocolate slightly.

Holding a strawberry by the stem, dip one side of the fruit into the melted chocolate and twist slightly to cover half the berry.

Place on baking sheet and continue with the remaining berries.

To set the chocolate, chill berries in refrigerator for about 15 minutes.

Melt the milk chocolate the same way as the dark chocolate. Dip the uncovered halves of the berries into the melted milk chocolate.

Place in refrigerator and chill for another 15 minutes.

Overnight Pecan Coffee Cake

MAKES ONE 8-INCH ROUND CAKE

2 cups	all-purpose flour
1 teaspoon	baking powder
1 teaspoon	baking soda
1 teaspoon	cinnamon
1 teaspoon	lemon zest
¼ teaspoon	salt
⅔ cup	butter
1 cup	white sugar
½ cup	brown sugar
3	eggs
1 cup	buttermilk
½ cup	brown sugar
1 cup	pecans, chopped
1 teaspoon	cinnamon

Grease or line with parchment paper an 8-inch round springform pan. In a mixing bowl, combine together flour, baking powder, baking soda, 1 teaspoon cinnamon, lemon zest and salt. Set aside.

In a mixer, cream together butter, white sugar and ½ cup brown sugar until fluffy. Add eggs one at a time until fully incorporated. To avoid lumps, mix on low speed. Add ½ of the flour mixture to the egg mixture until combined. Then add ½ cup of buttermilk and the remaining flour mixture until combined. Finally, add remaining buttermilk and combine. Do not overmix the batter. Place batter in prepared springform pan.

To make the topping, combine ½ cup brown sugar, pecans and cinnamon. Sprinkle topping over the cake batter. Cover with plastic wrap and refrigerate overnight (or bake immediately in a preheated 350°F oven for about 1 hour).

When you are ready to bake, preheat oven to 350°F. Place cake in oven and bake for about 1½ hours or until tester comes out clean.

Variations

Lemon Blueberry Coffee Cake

Fold in 1 cup blueberries and another teaspoon of lemon zest after the buttermilk.

Venetian Vanilla Breakfast Loaf

MAKES 1 LARGE LOAF

4	eggs, separated
1 cup	sugar
½ cup	olive oil
2 teaspoons	pure vanilla
2 tablespoons	orange zest
2 tablespoons	lemon zest
1⅓ cup	milk
1 tablespoon	baking powder
2¼ cups	all-purpose flour
3 tablespoons	cocoa powder

Preheat oven to 350°F. Grease or parchment-line a 9- x 5-inch loaf pan.

In a bowl, whisk together the yolks and ¾ cup of the sugar until the mixture is light, then whisk in oil, vanilla and the zests.

In a separate bowl, combine the milk and the baking powder. Stir in the yolk mixture.

In another bowl, beat the egg whites until stiff and add the remaining ¼ cup sugar, a little at a time, beating to create a meringue. Stir the flour into the milk mixture. Fold meringue gently into the batter.

In a small bowl, combine cocoa powder with ¼ cup of the batter.

Pour half the remaining batter into the loaf pan. Swirl (marble) the cocoa mixture into the batter. Pour the remaining batter overtop.

Bake for about 1 hour or until tester comes out clean. Cool for about 10 minutes.

Delicious served warm with a good cup of coffee. On a mother-daughter Venice trip I tasted a loaf very much like this one and have re-created it for this book.

Espresso Chocolate Loaf

MAKES 1 LARGE LOAF

1 cup	butter, softened
1 cup	brown sugar
1 tablespoon	pure vanilla
2	eggs, beaten
1 cup	semisweet chocolate chips, melted and slightly cooled
1 cup	strong coffee or espresso
1½ cups	all-purpose flour
1 teaspoon	baking powder
1 teaspoon	baking soda

Do not unmold loaf too early otherwise it will fall apart. This loaf freezes extremely well and the recipe can be easily doubled or tripled!

Preheat oven to 350°F. Grease well a 9- x 5-inch loaf pan.

In a mixer, cream together butter, brown sugar and vanilla. Add eggs slowly until fully incorporated. Add melted and slightly cooled chocolate and coffee.

In a separate bowl, mix together flour, baking powder and baking soda.

Gradually add the flour mixture to the chocolate/coffee mixture and, with whisk attachment in mixer, whisk until combined. Do not overmix.

Pour batter into loaf pan. Bake 50–60 minutes or until tester comes out clean.

Cool in pan for about 1 hour. Go around the edge of the loaf with a paring knife and gently turn loaf onto wire rack.

Viennese Apple Strudel

½ cup	breadcrumbs
⅓ cup	butter, melted
4	tart apples (Granny Smith), peeled, cored and sliced
½ cup	sugar
1 teaspoon	cinnamon
1 tablespoon	vanilla sugar
¼ cup	golden raisins
2 tablespoons	rum (optional)
4 tablespoons	almonds, sliced
6 sheets	phyllo dough (3 sheets for each strudel)
½ cup	butter, melted for brushing
	icing sugar to garnish

Preheat oven to 400°F.

In a saucepan, sauté the breadcrumbs in the butter until golden brown. Set aside.

In a bowl, mix apple slices with the sugar, cinnamon, vanilla sugar, raisins, rum (if using), almonds and sautéed breadcrumbs.

Place a tea towel on a working surface. Lightly spray with water. Place a sheet of phyllo onto the tea towel, generously butter it and then place 2 more phyllo sheets overtop.

Spread ½ the apple mixture on the top phyllo sheet, leaving a 2-inch border on each side. Fold in the phyllo edges about 2 inches on each side to seal in the apples. Grasp the far edge of the tea towel and pull it towards you over the strudel, rolling up the strudel into a log.

Transfer to a greased baking sheet or one lined with parchment paper. Make the second strudel using the same method. Brush both strudels with melted butter.

Bake for 40 minutes or until golden brown.

Thanks, Mom, for the great Austrian recipe – a family tradition!

Vanillekipferln
(Austrian Celebration Cookies)

MAKES 20 COOKIES

¾ cup	butter
3 tablespoons	icing sugar
heaping ¼ cup	almonds or walnuts, ground
1 cup	all-purpose flour
¾ cup	icing sugar
1 tablespoon	vanilla sugar

In a mixer, cream together the butter and icing sugar. Add the almonds and flour. Remove dough from mixer and form a log with the dough. Refrigerate for 1 hour.

Preheat oven to 375°F.

Cut the dough into 20 equal portions. Roll each slice into a small log, then form into a crescent. Place on parchment-lined cookie sheets and bake for about 10 minutes or until very light golden brown.

Make the topping by sifting together the icing sugar and vanilla sugar. While the crescents are still warm, roll in the vanilla-sugar mixture. Cool completely.

This easy but so delicious cookie is an Austrian Christmas tradition. At Fairholme we also make them for weddings or other special occasions.

Chocolate Icebox Cookies

MAKES 3 DOZEN COOKIES

½ cup	butter, room temperature
1 cup	brown sugar, lightly packed
1	egg
¼ cup	milk
2 cups	all-purpose flour
¾ cup	cocoa powder
1 teaspoon	baking powder
½ teaspoon	baking soda
½ teaspoon	salt

In a bowl, cream together the butter and brown sugar. Stir in the egg and milk.

In another bowl, sift together the flour, cocoa, baking powder, baking soda and salt.

Combine the butter mixture with the flour mixture and press into a disc. Cover and refrigerate dough for 1 hour or overnight.

Preheat oven to 350°F.

On a lightly floured work surface, roll the dough into an ⅛-inch thickness. Cut into mini star or heart shapes and transfer to parchment-lined cookie sheets.

Bake 6 minutes until the cookies are set. Cool on racks.

These cookies look great when nicely packaged and make perfect little gifts (page 144).

Coconut & Lime Cookies

MAKES ABOUT 40 COOKIES

¾ cup	butter, softened
¼ cup	brown sugar
1	egg yolk
2 teaspoons	pure vanilla
1 tablespoon	lime zest
1½ cups	all-purpose flour
1 cup	coconut, shredded
¼ cup	raw sugar to garnish

In a bowl, cream the butter with the sugars. Add the yolk, vanilla and lime zest. Stir in the flour and coconut.

Turn out the dough onto a lightly floured surface and roll into a 10-inch log. Roll log in raw sugar. Wrap in plastic wrap and refrigerate until firm, at least 2 hours.

Preheat oven to 350°F. Grease 2 cookie sheets or line with parchment paper.

Slice the chilled dough into ¼-inch rounds and place 1 inch apart on the cookie sheets.

Bake until edges are golden, about 10–15 minutes. Cool completely and serve.

This cookie packages well as an easy gift from the kitchen (see next page).

Little Gifts from the Kitchen

Hostess gifts from the kitchen are fun and easy to make.

Package cookies and granola in cellophane or rice paper, tied up with twine. Or perhaps wrap a large teacup in ribbon and fill it with mini scones.

So simple and chic!

Contributors

Mary Patterson
Food preparation

Mary was schooled at L'Ecole de Cuisine Française Sabine de Mirbeck in the UK and apprenticed at Le Mas d'Aigret in Provence. She has cooked and baked in Canadian west coast establishments, including the Metropolitan Hotel diner, Hastings House, Bishop's, Il Terrazzo, Rebar Modern Foods, Brasserie L'Ecole, the Italian Bakery and, of course, Fairholme Manor. Mary is author of the illustrated *Special Cookbook*.

John Archer of John Archer Photography
Food and Inn photography

John is based in Victoria, BC, and has specialized in wedding photography for the past 20 years. His style is a combination of photojournalism and glamour and fashion photography.
www.archerphotography.com

Cathie Ferguson of Cathie Ferguson Photography
Author and Inn photography

Cathie has been a Victoria-based photographer for the past 19 years, specializing in commercial and portrait work. She has travelled extensively and especially enjoys photographing interiors and architecture.
www.cathieferguson.com

Erica Smolders of
Rook & Rose Floral Design Boutique
Flowers

Erica began her floral design career in 2003 while attending art school in Perth, Australia. After nearly a decade of designing in flower shops across Vancouver Island and around the world she opened Rook & Rose, a luxury floral boutique located in the downtown fashion district of Victoria, BC. Here you can find her and her talented team creating stunning florals for weddings, special events and everyday occasions.
www.rookandrose.com

Photo by Red Leaf Studio

Sandy Reber of Reber Creative Design & Communications
Book design & layout

Sandy and her team have worked with Sylvia in the design and layout of both *Fabulous Fairholme* books. Sandy enjoys the collaborative approach and working closely with her clients to help them achieve (and exceed) their vision. In addition to books, her firm designs and edits a wide range of reports, marketing collateral and education materials.
www.reberco.com

Sue Frause
Foreword and selected editing

Sue is a freelance writer, photographer and radio correspondent. Her words and images appear online and in magazines, where she focuses on travel, food and colourful personalities. Sue's adventures have taken her to all seven continents, but her favourite place on the planet is home on Whidbey Island, with her husband Bob and their very own field of dreams.
www.closetcanuck.com

Ross Main
Additional photographs

Ross takes photos of Fairholme throughout the year and captures many special moments at the Inn. He has simple and beautiful taste, which is reflected in his photography. Guests love having Ross around with his good sense of humour, interesting stories and warm, likeable personality.

Index

About the Author

Sylvia Main was born and raised in Vienna, Austria, and moved to Canada with her family as a teenager. She has travelled extensively throughout Europe, where she is continually inspired by the lifestyle, beautiful surroundings and cuisine.

Some of Sylvia's fondest memories are the trips she made as a child with her family to local markets and farms in Europe.

In the kitchen, Sylvia likes to prepare food with seasonal, fresh and local ingredients, as she believes quality ingredients are key to fabulous results.

Sylvia and her husband, Ross, opened Fairholme Manor Inn in Victoria's Rockland area in 1999. The Italianate-style home was built in 1885 by Dr. John C. Davie, a medical pioneer and long-term provincial health officer. Fairholme is located adjacent to the gardens of Government House, the official residence of the Lieutenant Governor of British Columbia, the representative of Queen Elizabeth.

Sylvia and Ross have two daughters, Simone and Nicola. Sylvia's debut book, *Fabulous Fairholme: Breakfast & Brunches,* is a Canadian bestseller.